Express Your Big Emotions With No Hitting

Teaching Toddlers Self-Control

Grace Love, PhD

"Sometimes, kids want you to hurt the way they hurt."

-Mitch Albom

Table of Contents

Introduction

Toddlers are remarkable beings. They're so curious about the world around them, and even though they are able to understand thousands of words spoken to them, they might not be able to speak most of those words. A huge part of parenting a toddler is their tantrum phase! The tantrums and the crying are all part of the "terrible twos"—a phase in a toddler's life where they don't really understand their emotions. These first few years of a toddler's life are so important and a crucial time in their lives because this is when they start to learn social skills and how to interact with other children. They are also very observant at this stage and will often mimic behavior that they see from those around them.

I can understand how frustrating and exhausting these tantrums can be for you as parents and the toll it takes on your emotions and on your mental state of mind. As an experienced child psychologist and a mother of two, I have enough experience with children who have behavior issues, and I understand the psychology behind toddlers behaving badly. I have been an authoritative figure in these children's lives, and I have helped both parents and their children learn techniques to cope with their tantrums. As a parent, you would never want to walk around on eggshells around your toddler—hoping that they wouldn't suddenly blow up in a tantrum over something you had no control over.

I have been through this with my kids, and there were days where I just wanted to hide in my closet and not come out. But I can assure you that it all gets better in time; they do eventually grow out of it. Getting them to calm down can seem next to impossible, but if you use the right approach, you will be able to help your toddler calm down easily. This book will help you and your child to understand what the problems are and how to deal with them.

The first part of this book will bring awareness to your child about their behavior through a story. The second part of the book explains your child's behavior and helps you understand why these tantrums occur; the third part of the book gives you, the parent, strategies on how to deal with this type of behavior.

Part 1:

My Hands Don't Hit

We all have feelings! We can all feel happy, we can feel sad, we can feel angry, and we can feel scared. These are a lot of different feelings to have in such a little body. When you get angry with someone, you feel like hitting them.

Sometimes, you will feel sad and hit Mommy, or sometimes, you will feel angry and hit your teddy bears.

When your brother or sister does not want to play with you, you will feel mad and would want to hit.

Sometimes, when you are really tired and you need a nap, you would feel like hitting.

5

When your friend at day care does not want to share, that would make you feel like hitting, too.

When you feel like hitting, you feel big and scary feelings that keep growing and getting bigger inside you. You just want those feelings to come out, but you don't know how to take them out, and that makes you feel like hitting.

Hitting others is not good! It hurts others' feelings and makes them sad. You know that hitting is wrong. Hitting others can make them scared of you. They will feel very sad, and it would even make them cry. I know that you don't want to make your friends cry.

You love your mom, and you love your dad. You love your sister, your brother, and you love your friends also.

Grown-ups won't let you hit someone else. They will help you when you are feeling angry and sad. Grown-ups know that hitting is not allowed, and they will teach you not to hit others.

When you are feeling angry and you want to hit, you can tell your mommy or daddy about how you are feeling. Tell Mom, "I feel angry," or "I feel sad; can you help me, please?" Mommy will give you a big hug to take those big feelings of anger away. Daddy can take you for a short walk.

You can use your little hands to play with your toys.

You can use your little hands to clap along to your favorite song, and you can use your little hands to draw Mommy and Daddy a beautiful picture.

You can use your little hands to have fun and make others happy.

Part 2:

Understanding Your Child

A Guide for Parents

What Makes Your Toddler Want to Hit?

This is a confusing and complicated time for your toddler. They want to assert themselves and show how they are feeling. All of these emotions and feelings that they are experiencing are all new to them, so can you imagine how difficult it must be for them to have control over their feelings. Even some adults are not able to handle or control their feelings, so why would we expect our toddlers to be able to control their feelings? They don't understand the world, they are still discovering and learning every day. A toddler's emotions and feelings are still developing, and they have limited self-control at this stage in their lives. Your toddler doesn't understand that their hitting is hurting others. They don't have a sense of compassion because this only comes into place at around three years of age.

As your child continues to grow, there will be many changes that take place between 18 months and three years. It is important that you be patient and understanding toward your toddler, as they are becoming aware of themselves as individuals. During this phase, your toddler will want to communicate their feelings and hitting is common in toddlers—especially in the earlier stages. Between the ages of 12 and 24 months, you would notice a peak in their behavior, and hitting would start to develop during this time; it can continue between two to three years. It can get more difficult for parents during this phase since their toddlers are learning to talk better, and they will be able to understand basic rules. But even though they are aware, they still cannot control their feelings, and they would not be able to remember the rules in the moment.

Things That Trigger Hitting Behavior in Toddlers

There could be a number of different reasons why your toddler is hitting. They could be trying to communicate their needs with you.

Tired or Hungry

When they are tired or hungry, they may want to let you know, but they can't because their verbal skills have not been fully developed yet.

Defending Their Territory

Your toddler will defend their territory when other kids are invading their space and touching their toys.

Your Toddler Is Angry or Sad

When your toddler might be having a bad day, this could put them in a bad mood.

Imitating What They Have Seen

Your toddler may be imitating hitting behavior that they have seen at home or at school.

They Are Naturally Temperamental

If your toddler throws tantrums often and always hits, a good reason for this is that your toddler is temperamental.

Most of the time, hitting is a normal response to the aforementioned triggers, but sometimes, it can be traced back to something else, like the following:

- Early signs of a learning disability

- Problems within the family

- Emotional stress

- Lack of sleep

- Watching violence on TV

If you are concerned that your child may have a problem with aggression, look out for these signs:

- Always loses their temper often

- Their attention span is short compared to others

- Physically fights with other kids and adults

- Always disruptive and irritable

- Has trouble being social within a group

If your toddler displays these signs and if you don't see any improvement with the strategies that you are trying, then you should talk to your pediatrician. However, children do grow out of this behavior, so you can help them using the strategies given in the next section.

Part 3:

Practical Strategies to Prevent Your Child From Hitting Out

Three-Step Overview for Dealing With Hitting Behavior

Step 1: Watch and Learn

Observing your child can help you see any patterns and find underlying causes for their behavior. You can then decide on the best strategy to help your child.

What's Going on for Your Child?

Determine **where** the behavior is taking place:

- Is it at home or at school?

- Does it happen when you're out in public?

- Does it happen when your child is visiting a specific family member's home?

Determine **who** their behavior is directed toward:

- Is your child only behaving this way with a certain individual?

- Is your child behaving this way with anyone they come in contact with?

Determine **when** your child behaves this way:

- Does it happen when your child is tired?

- Does it happen before bedtime?

Does it happen during a bath?

Does it happen every day?

What's Going on for You?

- How do you feel when your child behaves this way?

- How do you cope with your feelings during this time?

- How do you respond to your child?

- Do you feel that your response is helping your child?

Step 2: Deal With the Behavior

Stay Calm

Take a few moments to yourself to let the frustration and anger phase out and to gather your thoughts. You need to be the secure rope that reels your child back in when they are angry or upset.

Recognize Your Child's Emotions and Intentions

Make your child know that you are there and that you understand what they want to do. "You want to play with your brother's toys, but hitting your brother is wrong."

Communicate With Your Child Using Gestures and Words

Use your voice in a firm, authoritative manner to let your child know that their behavior is bad and that they need to stop.

Step 3: Help Them Learn From Their Actions

Point Out Consequences

Help your child to understand that after they hit their friend or brother, that made their brother sad and he cried. Now, he does not want to play anymore.

Discuss Better Choices

Suggest some ideas to help your child deal with their feelings in a different manner the next time someone does something to upset them.

Remind Them You Are There to Help

Let your child know that they can always come to you for help no matter what; you will always be there to make things better.

Minimizing Behavior

There are strategies you can use to help minimize your toddler's behavior. Here are a few ways:

- Consistency: Establish rules and use consequences to reinforce them.

- Avoid negotiation.

Let the child have a go at resolving the problem.

Give positive feedback for self-control.

Dealing With Hitting Behavior in the Moment—What Not to Do:

• Try not to become aggressive yourself, as this could make things worse. Children observe others and mimic that behavior. Your child will not want to come to you for help if you show that you are angry or aggressive toward them.

• Don't use corporal punishment. Spanking makes things worse because it will confuse the child about hitting.

• Don't respond using a big reaction that your child may want to trigger again.

What You Can Do:

• Restrain your child if necessary.

• Remove your child from the situation. Going for a walk will help.

• Provide a distraction to help the child calm down.

• Provide an alternate way to deal with their feelings.

• Show empathy.

What You Can Do Immediately After the Behavior:

- Provide emotional support for your child. Help them understand that you will always be there to help them whenever they need you.

- Discuss the alternatives with your child. Teach your child about other ways they can use to express how they are feeling.

Planning Ahead to Prevent and Manage Their Behavior:

- Teach your child appropriate behavior and anger management skills.

- Promote and praise good self-control.

- Help them practice touching people softly.

- Teach them that feelings are different from actions.

- Create a positive time-out area and include your child in this.

- Model positive ways of dealing with emotions.

- Plan nap times and offer healthy snacks to reduce the chance of triggers.

- Tie their actions to another person's feelings.

- Teach problem-solving skills.

- Monitor their TV and Internet consumption.

Language and Phrases That You Can Use With Your Child:

"Hitting makes people sad."

- "Go for a time-out for 10 minutes because you broke the rules."

- "Take deep breaths whenever you feel angry."

"It's better to make someone smile than to make them cry."

- "Don't use your hands to hurt someone."

Conclusion

Remember that your toddler is discovering themselves and hitting is part of that phase. Your child's behavior will not change overnight, but when you work with them and implement these strategies that you have learned about, you will notice a change. Now you know exactly what to do the next time your child experiences big emotions; all that you have to do is be supportive and get to work.

If this book has helped you find answers and guidance with your child's hitting problem, then please leave us a review. Every parent goes through similar situations with their toddlers. Help them find the resources they need to live a happy life.

References

8 Phrases to Use When Disciplining to Your Child. (n.d.). Verywell Family. Retrieved Septembe 9, 2021, from https://www.verywellfamily.com/things-to-say-when-disciplining-your-children-4165520

Aggression, Ages 1 to 3. (2021a, July 31). Consumer Health News | HealthDay. https://consumer healthday.com/encyclopedia/children-s-health-10/child-development-news-124/aggression-ages-1-to-3-645129.html

Aggression, Ages 1 to 3. (2021b, July 31). Consumer Health News | HealthDay. https://consumer healthday.com/encyclopedia/children-s-health-10/child-development-news-124/aggression-ages-1-to-3-645129.html

Aggressive Behavior in Toddlers. (2016). ZERO to THREE. https://www.zerotothree.org resources/16-aggressive-behavior-in-toddlers

How to Stop a Toddler from Hitting. (n.d.-a). Parents. Retrieved September 9, 2021, from https:// www.parents.com/toddlers-preschoolers/development/behavioral/tough-toddlers-4-common-triggers-for-hitting-and-biting/

How to Stop a Toddler from Hitting. (n.d.-b). Parents. https://www.parents.com/toddlers-preschoolers/development/behavioral/tough-toddlers-4-common-triggers-for-hitting-and-biting/

Mitch Albom. (n.d.). AZQuotes.com. Retrieved from AZQuotes.com Web site: https://www.azquotes.com/quote/370110

Toddler Hitting: Why It Happens and How To Make It Stop. (2020, April 21). Healthline. https://www.healthline.com/health/parenting/toddler-hitting#what-to-do

Toddlers and the Hitting Stage. (2017, March 28). Www.positivediscipline.com. https://www.positivediscipline.com/articles/toddlers-and-hitting-stage